DIVERSITY

Compiled by
Dan Zadra and Kristel Wills

Designed by
Steve Potter and Jenica Wilkie

COMPENDIUM™
PUBLISHING

live inspired.

Acknowledgements

These quotations were gathered lovingly but unscientifically over several years and/or contributed by many friends or acquaintances. Some arrived—and survived in our files—on scraps of paper and may therefore be imperfectly worded or attributed. To the authors, contributors and original sources, our thanks, and where appropriate, our apologies. —The Editors

With Special Thanks To

Jason Aldrich, Gerry Baird, Jay Baird, Neil Beaton, Josie Bissett, Jan Catey, Doug Cruickshank, Jim Darragh, Jennifer & Matt Ellison, Rob Estes, Michael Flynn & Family, Shannan Frisbie, Jennifer Hurwitz, Heidi Jones, Cristal & Brad Olberg, Janet Potter & Family, Diane Roger, Jenica Wilkie, Clarie Yam & Erik Lee, Kobi, Heidi & Shale Yamada, Justi, Tote & Caden Yamada, Robert & Val Yamada, Kaz, Kristin, Kyle & Kendyl Yamada, Tai & Joy Yamada, Anne Zadra, August & Arline Zadra.

Credits

Compiled by Dan Zadra and Kristel Wills
Designed by Steve Potter and Jenica Wilkie

Celebrating the Differences

DIVERSITY

We are all unique, and if that is not fulfilled,
then something wonderful has been lost.

Martha Graham

There has never been another you. There are more than
six billion people on earth. Linked arm-in-arm the entire
human family would form a multi-colored chain that would
stretch to the moon and back several times. And yet,
not one of those individuals possesses your exact same
combination of background, ideas, feelings, intuitions
and potential answers.

Simply put, you are as unique as your own fingerprint.
There has never been another you, and there will never be

another you. Therefore, no one can really predict to what heights you might soar.

The people quoted in these pages would probably all agree that you are not here by mistake. In a world where there is much to be done, you have a gift that only you can give. We need your unique answers, ideas and contributions—and you need ours.

In today's rapidly shrinking world we are either pulling together or we are pulling apart; there's really no in between.

"We are all unique," reminds Martha Graham, "and if that is not fulfilled, then something wonderful has been lost."

Dan Zadra

Be yourself; everyone else is already taken.

OSCAR WILDE

DIVERSITY

The individual is the central, rarest, most
precious capital resource of our society.

PETER F. DRUCKER

We are all born with wonderful gifts. We use these
gifts to express ourselves, to amuse, to strengthen,
and to communicate. We begin as children to explore
and develop our talents, often unaware that we are
unique, that not everyone can do what we're doing!

LYNN JOHNSTON

Every man and woman is born into the world to do something unique and something distinctive, and if he or she does not do it, it will never be done.

BENJAMIN E. MAYS

At bottom everyone knows well enough that he or she is a unique being, only once on this earth; and by no extraordinary chance will such a marvelously picturesque piece of diversity in unity ever be put together a second time.

FRIEDRICH NIETZSCHE

Insist on yourself; never imitate.

RALPH WALDO EMERSON

I didn't belong as a kid, and that always
bothered me. If only I'd known that one
day my differentness would be an asset,
my earlier life would have been much easier.

BETTE MIDLER

Be who you are, and say what you feel,
because those who mind don't matter,
and those who matter don't mind.

DR. SEUSS

You are unique,
and if that is
not fulfilled,
then something
wonderful has
been lost.

MARTHA GRAHAM

DIVERSITY

Everyone, including and perhaps
especially you, is indispensable.

NATHANIEL HAWTHORNE

Every individual matters.
Every individual has a role to play.
Every individual makes a difference.

MOTTO OF THE JANE GOODALL INSTITUTE

You are here for a purpose. There is not a duplicate of you
in the whole wide world; there never has been, there never
will be. You were brought here now to fill a certain need.
Take time to consider what it might be.

LOU AUSTIN

Whatever you are, be a good one.

ABRAHAM LINCOLN

Don't let anyone rob you of your imagination,
your creativity, or your curiosity. It's your place
in the world; it's your life. Go on and do all you
can with it, and make it the life you want to live.

MAE JEMISON

Be a first-rate version of yourself,
not a second-rate version of someone else.

JUDY GARLAND

We have the right and the incredible opportunity
to develop our own separate individualities in the
pursuit of happiness, not only for ourselves but for
those we love, for our teammates or colleagues,
for our community, and the world in general.

GEOFF BURNETT

You have a gift that only you can give to the world—
that's the whole reason you're on the planet.
Use your precious energy to build a magnificent
life that really is attainable. The miracle of your
existence calls for celebration every day.

OPRAH WINFREY

You have a creative contribution to make. Our lives will be better if you do.

MICHAEL TOMS

In a world where there is so much to be done,
I felt strongly impressed that there must be
something for me to do.

DOROTHEA DIX

If you want to be truly successful, invest in yourself to
get the knowledge you need to find your unique factor.
When you find it and focus on it and persevere,
your success will blossom.

SYDNEY MADWED

Just be yourself. Above all,
let who you are, what you are,
what you believe, shine through.

JOHN JAKES

We are all born originals—
why is it so many of us die copies?

EDWARD YOUNG

When we die and go to heaven, our Maker
is not going to say, why didn't you discover
the cure for such and such? The only thing
we're going to be asked at that precious
moment is why didn't you become you?

ELIE WIESEL

What you have, what you are—
your looks, your personality, your way
of thinking—is unique. No one in the
world is like you, so capitalize on it.

JACK LORD

Know that you yourself are a miracle.

NORMAN VINCENT PEALE

We are not powerless specks of dust drifting
around in the wind, blown by random destiny.
We are, each of us, like beautiful snowflakes—
unique, and born for a specific reason and purpose.

ELIZABETH KUBLER-ROSS

If we did all the things we are capable of,
we would literally astound ourselves.

THOMAS EDISON

Where all think alike, no one thinks very much.

WALTER LIPPMANN

DIVERSITY

Originality exists in every individual because each of us differs from the other. We are all prime numbers divisible only by ourselves.

JEAN GUITTON

We grow up thinking that the best answer is in someone else's brain. Much of our education is an elaborate game of "guess what's in the teacher's head?" What the world really needs to know right now is what kind of unique dreams and ideas are in your head.

ROGER VON OECH

We know what we are,
but know not what we may be.

WILLIAM SHAKESPEARE

We all have the extraordinary coded
within us, waiting to be released.

J.L. HOUSTON

Everyone has inside him a piece of good news.
The good news is that you don't yet realize
how great you can be! How much you can love!
What you can accomplish! And what your potential is!

ANNE FRANK

Each second we live is a new and unique moment of the universe, a moment that will never be again. And what do we teach our children? We teach them that two and two make four, and that Paris is the capital of France. When will we also teach them what they are? We should say to each of them: Do you know what you are? You are a marvel. You are unique. In all the years that have passed, there has never been another child like you. Your legs, your arms, your clever fingers, the way you move. You may become a Shakespeare, a Michelangelo, a Beethoven. You have the capacity for anything.

PABLO PICASSO

Treat all people with dignity and respect.

JOHN WOODEN

DIVERSITY

Nowadays, the common wisdom is to celebrate diversity—as long as you don't point out that people are different.

COLIN QUINN

You can make your world so much larger simply by acknowledging everyone else's.

JEANNE MARIE LASKAS

Brilliance comes in all colors, strengths in many forms. When we learn to honor the differences and appreciate the mix, we're on our way.

KELLY ANN ROTHAUS

23

Always keep an open mind and
a compassionate heart.

PHIL JACKSON

If we could look into each other's hearts and
understand the unique challenges each of us face,
I think we would treat each other much more gently,
with more love, patience, tolerance, and care.

MARVIN J. ASHTON

Compassion and respect for yourself translates
into compassion and respect for others.

SUKI JAY MUNSELL

Every person is a new door to a different world.

"SIX DEGREES OF SEPARATION"

It's the things in common that make
relationships enjoyable, but it's the
differences that make them interesting.

TODD RUTHMAN

Just when you think that a person is just a
backdrop for the rest of the universe, watch
them and see that they laugh, they cry, they
tell jokes...they're just friends waiting to be made.

DR. JEFFREY BORENSTEIN

They are the same heart.

JAMES McBRIDE

DIVERSITY

We all live with the objective of being happy; our lives are all different and yet the same.

ANNE FRANK

We may not always see eye to eye,
but we can try to see heart to heart.

SAM LEVENSON

He drew a circle that shut me out; heretic, rebel,
a thing to flout. But love and I had the will to win;
we drew a circle that took him in.

EDWIN MARKHAM

I am a part of all that I have met.

ALFRED, LORD TENNYSON

Tolerance is the greatest gift of the mind;
it requires the same effort of the brain
that it takes to balance oneself on a bicycle.

HELEN KELLER

One day our descendants will think it incredible
that we paid so much attention to things like the
amount of melanin in our skin, or the shape of
our eyes, or our gender, instead of the unique
identities of each of us as complex human beings.

FRANKLIN THOMAS

Each person wants a voice in human freedom—
the freedom to express our individuality in work
and life. That's a fire burning inside all of us.

LECH WALESA

Listening to contemporary music, you may hear an artist who
is blind. If you prefer classical, you may enjoy a symphony
written by a composer who couldn't hear. The president who
set an unbeatable American political record could hardly
walk. A woman born unable to see, speak or hear stands as
a great achiever in American history. The [differently-abled]
among us have enriched our lives. Let's enrich theirs.

GREY MATTER

There is greatness all around you—welcome it! It is easy to be great when you get around great people.

BOB RICHARDS

DIVERSITY

Discover what is unique, what is great,
about people and honor it, be happy for it, use it.

JOHN BUNN

There comes that mysterious meeting in life
when someone acknowledges who we are
and what we can be, igniting the circuits of
our highest potential.

RUSTY BERKUS

Really great people make you feel
that you, too, can become great.

MARK TWAIN

I love different folks.

ELEANOR H. PORTER

Truly loving another means letting go
of all expectations. It means full acceptance,
even celebration of another's personhood.

KAREN CASEY

It's so clear that you have to cherish everyone.
I think that's what I get from these older black
women, that every soul is to be cherished,
that every flower is to bloom.

ALICE WALKER

We pass the word around; we ponder how the case is put by different people; we read the poetry; we meditate over the literature; we play the music; we change our minds; we reach an understanding. Society evolves this way, not by shouting each other down, but by the unique capacity of unique, individual human beings to comprehend and appreciate each other.

LEWIS THOMAS

We are here, charged with the task of
completing (one might say creating) ourselves.

WILLIAM COOK

The goal is not to make women more like
men, or men more like women, but for
everyone to become most like themselves.

ELEANOR BRANTLEY SCHWARTZ

Yes, we are all different. Different customs, foods,
mannerisms and languages, but not so different after
all...if we will disagree without being disagreeable.

J. MARTIN KOHE

You don't get harmony when
everybody sings the same note.

DOUG FLOYD

Your neighbor's vision is as true for him
as your own vision is true for you.

MIGUEL DE UNAMUNO

Our life is composed, like the harmony of the world,
of contrary things, also of different tones, sweet and
harsh, sharp and flat, soft and loud. If a musician
liked only one kind, what would he have to say?

MICHEL DE MONTAIGNE

I'm good; you're good. Together we're better.

DICK PERL

DIVERSITY

We don't accomplish anything in this world alone...
and whatever happens is the result of the whole
tapestry of one's life and all the weavings of individual
threads from one to another that creates something.

SANDRA DAY O'CONNOR

If I just do my thing and you do yours,
we stand in danger of losing each other
and ourselves. I must begin with myself,
true; but I must not end with myself.
The truth begins with two.

WALTER TUBBS

All men are caught in an
inescapable network of mutuality.

MARTIN LUTHER KING, JR.

We cannot live only for ourselves.
A thousand fibers connect us with our
fellow man; and along these fibers,
as sympathetic threads, our actions run
as causes, and they come back as effects.

HERMAN MELVILLE

Culture is a quilt of intricate geometrical
design in which all of the many colored pieces,
their shapes and stitching, flow into one another
constituting the other.

FRANCES CRESS WELSING

We are members one of another;
so that you cannot injure or help your
neighbor without injuring or helping yourself.

GEORGE BERNARD SHAW

Some people weave cotton into the fabric
of our lives, and some weave gold thread.
Both contribute to make the whole picture
beautiful and unique.

UNKNOWN

There is a place for everyone in the big picture.
To turn your back on any one person, for whatever
reason, is to run the risk of losing the central
piece of your jigsaw puzzle.

JOHNNA HOWELL

What a world this would be if we just built bridges instead of walls.

CARLOS RAMIREZ

DIVERSITY

Only connect.

E.M. FORSTER

The word communication comes from the
Latin *communico* meaning, "to come together."

DON WARD

True communication is an open bridge that
works both ways. When we build bridges
we can keep crossing them.

JANE ALVAREZ

Draw strength from each other.

JAMES A. RENIER

As a kid I learned that by taking the hand of my friend across the railroad track and by looking at the same horizon, we both could walk for miles without falling.

RAY KROC

United we stand, divided we fall.

AESOP

The most important ingredient we put into
any relationship is not what we say or what
we do, but what and who we are.

STEPHEN COVEY

Extending your hand is extending yourself.

ROD McKUEN

I hadn't set out to change the world in any way.
Whatever I am, it is a culmination of the goodwill
of people who, regardless of anything else,
saw me as I am, and not as somebody else.

MARIAN ANDERSON

There is somebody
smarter than any
of us, and that is
all of us.

MICHAEL NOLAN

DIVERSITY

No matter what accomplishments
you make, somebody helps you.

WILMA RUDOLPH

Every individual is capable of extraordinary things,
but no one can accomplish anything by themselves.

KAREN NUSSBAUM

No one can be the best at everything.
But when all of us combine our talents,
we can be the best at virtually anything.

DAN ZADRA

Your spark can become a flame
and change everything.

E.D. NIXON

In everyone's life, at some time,
our inner fire is burst into flame by
an encounter with another human being.

ALBERT SCHWEITZER

If I had to describe something as divine
it would be what happens between people
when they really get it together. There is a
kind of spark that makes it all worthwhile.
When you feel that spark, you get a good
feeling deep in your gut.

JUNE L. TAPP

The world is wide, and I will not
waste my life in friction when it
could be turned into momentum.

FRANCES WILLARD

There is a vitality, a life force, an energy,
a quickening, that is translated through you
into action, and because there is only one
of you in all time, this expression is unique.

MARTHA GRAHAM

When different talents and ideas rub up against
each other, there is friction, yes. But also sparks,
fire, light and—eventually—brilliance!

NANCIE O'NEILL

Encourage each
other to become
the best you can
be. Celebrate
what you want
to see more of.

TOM PETERS

We all need each other.

LEO BUSCAGLIA

Men and women are like right
and left hands; it doesn't make sense
not to use and appreciate both.

JEANNETTE RANKIN

Leave no one out of the big picture. As a rule
of thumb, involve everyone in everything of
any consequence to all of you.

TOM PETERS

Let's place a high value on
unity rather than uniformity.

DWIGHT D. EISENHOWER

If everyone is thinking alike,
then somebody isn't thinking.

GENERAL GEORGE S. PATTON

People take different roads seeking fulfillment
and happiness. Just because they're not on
your road doesn't mean they've gotten lost.

H. JACKSON BROWN

I hate categories.
I think they demean people.

QUINCY JONES

Instead of this absurd division
into sexes they ought to class
people as static or dynamic.

EVELYN WAUGH

If there must be a stereotype, let it have nothing
to do with race, creed, color, gender or advantage.
Let it have everything to do with effort, energy,
ideas, commitment and capabilities.

DAN ZADRA

Seeking diversity automatically leads us to excellence, just as focusing on excellence inevitably leads us to diversity.

WILLIAM C. STEERE

DIVERSITY

What if we could learn to tap the wonderful, rich differences among people? Wouldn't a corporation that could exploit the uniqueness of each of its employees be phenomenally powerful?

TOM PETERS

A symphony may be played by a hundred musicians responsive under the baton of a master conductor, or by fifty thousand mechanics playing a blueprint score.

WILLIAM J. CAMERON

Diversity: The art of thinking
independently together.

MALCOLM FORBES

Diversity is a competitive advantage.
Different people approach similar
problems in different ways.

RICH McGINN

It's a mistake to surround yourself only with
people just like you. Throw off that worn comforter—
and replace it with a crazy quilt of different and
imaginative people. Then watch the ideas erupt!

BETTY BENDER

Accepting diversity enables us to see that each of us is needed. It also enables us to abandon ourselves to the strengths of others, acknowledging that we cannot know or do everything on our own.

MAX DEPREE

Cacophony, Inc., a wild mixture of individual colors, sexes, styles, and ages, will almost automatically generate and pursue more interesting ideas than Homogeneity, Inc.

TOM PETERS, "THE PURSUIT OF WOW"

The most successful companies, communities and nations will be those that are willing to learn from others. From diversity will come creative fusion. And creative fusion will become a strategic tool in the era of global competition.

SHERIDAN TATSUNO

What Diversity "problem"? Diversity creates one and only one thing: opportunity.

TOM PETERS

What people often mean by getting rid of conflict is getting rid of diversity, and it is of the utmost importance that these should not be considered the same.

MARY PARKER FOLLETT

We need to reach that happy stage of our development when differences and diversity are not seen as sources of division and distrust, but of strength and inspiration.

JOSEFA ILOILO

The great organizations are those that celebrate the differences. They seek harmony, not uniformity. They hire talent, not color. They strive for oneness, not sameness.

GIL ATKINSON

We need diversity of thought in the
world to face the new challenges.

TIM BERNERS LEE

Each of us possesses a creative self.
The ultimate creative act is to express what
is most authentic and individual about you.

EILEEN M. CLEGG

Business needs a rush of serious creativity.
Creativity is, invariably, a byproduct of sparks
and new views. How does a company
acquire those assets? Diversity!

TOM PETERS

The great and invigorating influences in American life have been the unorthodox: the people who challenge an existing institution or way of life, or say and do things that make people think.

WILLIAM O. DOUGLAS

Be daring, be different, be impractical, be anything that will assert integrity of purpose and imaginative vision against the play-it-safers, the creatures of the commonplace, the slaves of the ordinary.

CECIL BEATON

The best hope
of solving all our
problems lies in
harnessing the
diversity, the energy
and the creativity of
all our people.

ROGER WILKINS

DIVERSITY

I believe in individuals banding together for a higher purpose. Some people don't like organizations. But it is always awesome to me when you can pool a lot of people who have so many diverse talents. That's when you can really make your program move.

HORTENSE CANADY

We provide an inclusive work environment that involves everyone and every idea and allows each employee to reach their potential. Our customers come from various countries, cultures and backgrounds; our employees should be no different.

"DIVERSITY STATEMENT," WHIRLPOOL

The best companies assume that each individual wants to make a difference in the world and be respected. Is that a surprise?

PAUL AMES

Wise leaders know that if an individual doesn't count, the company or organization doesn't count for much either. Put mathematically, if the individual is a zero, together a lot of zeros add up to a whole lot of nothing.

DIANE DREHER

I think that every person wants to make a genuine contribution in their lives, and one of the main vehicles to achieving this is their company and their work. I'm convinced that company leaders can create a diverse human community that will change our world.

WARREN BENNIS

Each of us brings to our job, whatever it is,
our lifetime of experience and our values.

SANDRA DAY O'CONNOR

My weakness may be your strength,
and vice versa. When we work as a team,
the strengths cancel the weaknesses. The result
is mutual respect throughout the entire team.

MIKE POWER

Cooperation is working together agreeably.
Collaboration is working together aggressively;
and there's a world of difference between the two.

JOHN C. MAXWELL

Ideas bring people together,
but ideals hold them together.

BILL MEYER

Imagine what a harmonious world it could
be if every single person both young and old
shared a little of what he is good at doing.

QUINCY JONES

Give me some young tigers who believe
anything is possible, and some old warriors
who will speak up for our cherished ideals.

HANNIBAL'S REDUX

A company or a team needs to be constantly rejuvenated by the infusion of young blood. It needs young people with the imagination and the guts to turn everything upside down if they can. It also needs old fogies to keep them from turning upside down those things that ought to be right side up. Above all, it needs young rebels and old conservatives who can work together, challenge each other's values, yield or hold fast with equal grace, and continue after each hard-fought battle to respect each other.

"BUILDING COMMUNITY"

Let us begin to see the true promise of our country and community, not as a melting pot, but as a kaleidoscope.

ROBERT F. KENNEDY

DIVERSITY

Community is a group of individuals that
is greater than the sum of its parts.

MARK SOFIELD

I perceive the world as a kaleidoscope.
The brighter each particle shines,
the better for society as a whole and
for each ethnic component in it.

THEODORE BIKEL

Each of us puts in one little stone, and
then you get a great mosaic at the end.

ALICE PAUL

Each of us is connected to all living
things whether we are aware of
this beautiful fact or not.

GERALD JAMPOLSKY

Humankind has not woven the web of life.
We are but one thread within it. Whatever we
do to the web, we do to ourselves. All things
are bound together. All things connect.

CHIEF SEALTH

There's a thread that binds all of us together.
Pull one end of the thread, and the strain
is felt all down the line.

ROSAMOND MARSHALL

We have to find ways of organizing
ourselves with the rest of humanity.
It has to be everybody or nobody.

BUCKMINSTER FULLER

Science has made the world a neighborhood,
but it will take love to make it a sisterhood,
a brotherhood, a community of peace with justice.

ELIZABETH M. SCOTT

The whole idea of compassion is based on
a keen awareness of the interdependence
of all living beings, which are all part of
one another and all involved in one another.

THOMAS MERTON

Let us put our minds together and see what we will make for our children.

SITTING BULL

DIVERSITY

There is no such thing as
other people's children.

HILLARY RODHAM CLINTON

Civilization is the process of gradually increasing
the number of people included in the term "we"
or "us" while decreasing those labeled "you" or
"them" until that category has no one left in it.

HAROLD WINTER

When Christ asked little children to come to
him, He didn't say only rich children, or white
children, or children with two-parent families,
or children who didn't have a handicap.
He said, "Let all children come unto me."

MARIAN WRIGHT EDELMAN

A community is a group of people who have come together, and they work and they live to try and improve the standard of living and quality of life—and I don't mean money.

WILLIAM BALDWIN

When the term "community" is used, the notion that typically comes to mind is a place in which people know and care for one another—the kind of place in which people do not merely ask, "How are you?" as a formality, but care about the answer.

AMITAI ETZIONI

What is the city but the people?

WILLIAM SHAKESPEARE

We are a nation of neighborhoods and communities—
a brilliant diversity spread like stars, like a thousand
points of light in a broad and peaceful sky.

GEORGE H. W. BUSH

To live in a society doesn't mean simply living
side by side with others in a more or less close
cohesion; it means living through one another
and for one another.

PAUL-EUGENE ROY

There are no problems
we cannot solve
together, and very
few we can solve
by ourselves.

LYNDON B. JOHNSON

DIVERSITY

Lesson: People who share a common direction and sense of community can get where they're going quicker and easier because they're traveling on the strength of one another.

GREAT NORTHERN GEESE, LESSON 1

Nearly every problem our world faces is currently being solved in some community by some group or some individual. Imagine what might happen if we could only get all these hearts and minds connected so that we could collectively tackle our problems.

DIANE BRANSON

An individual has not started living until he can
rise above the narrow confines of his individualistic
concerns to the broader concerns of all humanity.

MARTIN LUTHER KING, JR.

Snowflakes, leaves, humans, plants, raindrops,
stars, molecules, microscopic entities all come in
communities. The singular cannot in reality exist.

PAULA GUNN ALLEN

While we may be of different faiths, we have a
strong sense of faith, family, community. We hold
the values of freedom and human rights very high,
and I think that those are all a part of a very strong
quilt that binds us together.

ROBERT MENENDEZ

We were born to unite with
our fellow men, and to join in
community with the human race.

CICERO

What do we live for, if not to make
life less difficult for each other?

GEORGE ELIOT

Wherever I have knocked, a door opened.
Wherever I have wandered, a path appeared.
I have been helped, supported, encouraged,
and nurtured by people of all races, creeds,
colors, and dreams.

ALICE WALKER

If we have not peace, it is because we have forgotten that we belong to each other.

MOTHER TERESA

DIVERSITY

I note the obvious differences
between each sort and type,
but we are more alike, my friends,
than we are unalike.

MAYA ANGELOU

Being the only non-black was a unique experience.
After a few weeks, you're not aware of skin color
differences. You see the color; you're not blind,
but it doesn't matter. You see the human being first.

RICARDO MONTALBAN

We may have different religions,
different languages, different-colored skin,
but we all belong to one human race.

KOFI ANNAN

Then I saw you through myself,
and found that we were identical.

FAKHR AD-DIN

People are much more similar to one another
than they are different. We are all family.

ROGER PERKINS

With all human beings and all things
we shall be as relatives.

SIOUX INDIAN

We are one big family of people,
trying to make our way through
the unfolding puzzle of life.

SARA PADDISON

Everyone carries with them at least
one piece to someone else's puzzle.

LAWRENCE KUSHNER

To see brotherhood in action, just watch a bunch
of high-school kids taking a final exam. There's no
question of race, creed, or color. There is only
one question: "Who's got the answer?"

SAM LEVENSON

We are, of course, a nation of differences. Those differences don't make us weak. They're the source of our strength.

JIMMY CARTER

DIVERSITY

Once I thought to write a history of the immigrants in America. Then I discovered that the immigrants were American history.

OSCAR HANDLIN

We didn't all come over in the same ship, but we're all in the same boat.

BERNARD M. BARUCH

We are a nation of immigrants. It is immigrants who brought to this land the skills of their hands and brains to make of it a beacon of opportunity and of hope for all.

HERBERT H. LEHMAN

Our country was founded in large part by immigrants, and they helped pave the way for all Americans to live in a country that values liberty and freedom. The greatness of our country stems from its diversity.

DIANE WATSON

This was the secret of America: a nation of people with the fresh memory of old traditions who dared to explore new frontiers, people eager to build lives for themselves in a spacious society that did not restrict their freedom of choice and action.

JOHN F. KENNEDY

Whatever we have been able to achieve has been
the result of the inherent harmony of the inheritance
which we have received from other cultures...
not merely in what is called the West, but in
what is called the East as well.

ERWIN D. CARHAM

We are the only country in the world that has taken
people from so many different backgrounds, which
is a great achievement by itself, but an even greater
achievement is that we have turned all of that variety
and diversity into unity.

LAMAR ALEXANDER

Accomplishments have no color, no gender.

LEONTYNE PRICE

Our flag is red, white and blue, but our nation is a rainbow—red, yellow, brown, black and white—and we're all precious in God's sight. America is not like a blanket—one piece of unbroken cloth, the same color, the same texture, the same size. America is more like a quilt—many patches, many pieces, many colors, many sizes, all woven and held together by a common thread.

REV. JESSE JACKSON

America is not just a country,
it's an idea.

BONO

America is not just a power, it is a promise.
It is not enough for a country to be extraordinary
in might; it must be exemplary in meaning.
Our honor in the world depends on the living
proof that we are a just society for all.

NELSON ROCKEFELLER

The idea that 280 million men and women
of different colors, backgrounds and nationalities
could live and work productively together in
peace and freedom is nothing but a dream—
the American Dream. Hold on to it.

GIL ATKINSON

We hold these truths to be self-evident,
that all men—and women—are created equal.

ELIZABETH CADY STANTON

I am not belittling the brave pioneer men,
but the sunbonnet as well as the sombrero
has helped to settle this glorious land of ours.

EDNA FERBER

We mothered this nation.
And we have no intention of abandoning our
roles as nurturer or wife, mother, loving daughter,
tax-paying citizen, homemaker and breadwinner.

LIZ CARPENTER

There is no
"them and us."
In a world this size
there can only be
"we"—all of us
working together.

DAN ZADRA

DIVERSITY

We believe we must be the family of America,
recognizing that at the heart of the matter
we are bound one to another.

MARIO CUOMO

For too long we've been told about "us" and
"them." Each and every election we see a
new slate of arguments and ads telling us that
"they" are the problem, not "us." But there
can be no "them" in America.

BILL CLINTON

Our country is not anything if it consists
of each of us. It is something only if
it consists of all of us.

WOODROW WILSON

America is too great for small dreams.

RONALD REAGAN

Our country just works better when more
people have a chance to live their dreams.

BILL CLINTON

Dreams, opportunity and dedication are
a powerful combination for good.

JAMES BEECHER

I look forward confidently to the day when all who work for a living will be one with no thought to their separateness as Negroes, Jews, Italians or any other distinctions. This will be the day when we shall bring into full realization the American dream, a dream yet unfulfilled...a dream of a land where men will not argue that the color of a man's skin determined the content of his character; a dream of a nation where all our gifts and resources are held not for ourselves alone, but as instruments of service for the rest of humanity; the dream of a country where every man will respect the dignity and worth of the human personality— that is the dream.

MARTIN LUTHER KING, JR.

We have become not a melting pot but
a beautiful mosaic. Different people, different beliefs,
different yearnings, different hopes, different dreams.

JIMMY CARTER

No one flower can ever symbolize this nation.
America is a bouquet.

WILLIAM SAFIRE

We really are 15 countries, and it's remarkable that
each of us thinks we represent the real America.
The Midwesterner in Kansas, the black American in
Durham—both are certain they are the real American.

MAYA ANGELOU

The happy ending is our national belief.

MARY McCARTHY

We as a people, as a state, and as a community,
have too much promise, too much potential,
and too much at stake to go any other way than
forward. We are too strong in our hearts, too
innovative in our minds, and too firm in our
beliefs to retreat from our goals.

BILL RICHARDSON

We must strive to ensure that the United States is a
nation that continues to value diversity, where we
stand together as one people, as equal people.

LEONARD BOSWELL

The age of nations has past. The task before us now is to build the Earth.

TEILHARD DE CHARDIN

Above all nations is humanity.

GOLDWIN SMITH

On this shrunken globe,
men can no longer live as strangers.

ADLAI E. STEVENSON

There are no passengers on Spaceship Earth.
Everybody's crew.

MARSHALL McLUHAN

When you're flying in space you get a much broader perspective of the world we live in. You recognize very quickly that this planet we live on is a small planet and we have to share it together. You recognize the importance of our managing our resources as effectively as possible, as well as the importance of getting along together.

GUION S. BUFORD

To see the Earth as we now see it, small and beautiful in that eternal silence where it floats, is to see ourselves as riders on the Earth together, brothers on that bright loveliness in the unending night—brothers who see how they are truly brothers.

ARCHIBALD MACLEISH

From space, I saw Earth—indescribably beautiful
with the scars of national boundaries gone.

MUHAMMAD AHMAD FARIS, SYRIA

The first day or so we all pointed to our countries.
The third or fourth day we were pointing to our continents.
By the fifth day we were aware of only one Earth.

SULTAN BIN SALMAN AL-SAUD, SAUDI ARABIA

For those who have seen the Earth from space, and for
the hundreds and perhaps thousands more who will,
the experience most certainly changes your perspective.
The things that we share in our world are far more
valuable than those which divide us.

DONALD WILLIAMS

No matter what
language we speak,
we all live under
the same moon
and stars.

JOHN DENVER

DIVERSITY

The whole world looks like home to me.

DAN ZADRA

Those are the same stars, and that is the same moon,
that look down upon your brothers and sisters, and
which they see as they look up to them, though they
are ever so far away from us, and each other.

SOJOURNER TRUTH

The love of one's country is a splendid thing.
But why should love stop at the border?

PABLO CASALS

Whether or not interplanetary communications ever materialize, an even more grandiose project awaits us. This is the need for human beings to communicate with one another, here and now.

NORMAN COUSINS

We live in a world in which isolation is no longer possible. We live in a time of unprecedented mobility of peoples and intermingling of cultures. We are all interdependent and share an inescapable responsibility for the well-being of the entire world.

UNESCO

Where we had thought to be alone,
we shall be with all the world.

JOSEPH CAMPBELL

Everyone's life, wherever lived, is now lived
in a global context. Societies which once
felt able to stand alone now see themselves
interlocked with others. The great human
goals of peace, justice, and prosperity are
now understood to require ever-widening
cooperative effort for their achievement.

BOUTROS BOUTROS-GHALI

I don't care what problems we have in the world—they can be solved by people coming together and organizing.

DOLORES HUERTA

DIVERSITY

My country is the world,
and my religion is to do good.

THOMAS PAINE

All of us have in us the spirit that unites all life and
everything that is on this planet. I am sure it's the same
voice that is speaking to everybody on this planet—
at least everybody who seems to be concerned about
the fate of the world, the fate of this planet.

WANGARI MAATHAI,
NOBEL PEACE PRIZE RECIPIENT

The start to a better world is
the belief that it is possible.

KATHERINE SHAW

I never thought I was going to save
the world, but I felt that I could work
and make some contribution to make things
better for people who come after me.

CORETTA SCOTT KING

I am trying to teach my children to feel
a responsibility for their fellow human
beings and a sense of connection with
the world around them.

GLORIA ESTEFAN

"We" rather than "I."

CHARLES GARFIELD

I must admit that I personally measure success
in terms of the contributions an individual makes
to her or his fellow human beings.

MARGARET MEAD

I now understand that my welfare is only
possible if I acknowledge my unity with all
the people of the world without exception.

LEO TOLSTOY

The most powerful and practical thing in the
world is common sense and common humanity.

NANCY ASTOR

Never before has man had such capacity to end
thirst and hunger, to conquer poverty and disease,
to banish illiteracy. We have the power to make
this the best generation of mankind in the history
of the world—or to make it the last.

JOHN F. KENNEDY

When spider webs unite,
they can tie up a lion.

ETHIOPIAN PROVERB

Think globally, but act locally.

RENE DUBOS

Somewhere on this planet, someone has a solution
to each of the world's problems. It might be one of us.
With your help, we can build a more hopeful world.

MARIANNE LARNED

One country, one ideology, one system
is not sufficient. It is helpful to have a
variety of different approaches. We can
then make a joint effort to solve the problems
of the whole of humankind.

THE DALAI LAMA

The opportunity to practice brotherhood presents itself every time you meet a human being.

JANE WYMAN

DIVERSITY

Kids know nothing of racism.
We as adults teach them.

RUBY BRIDGES HALL

Setting an example is not the main means
of influencing another, it is the only means.

ALBERT EINSTEIN

The most important gift anyone can give a
child is a belief in her own power as an
individual, her value without reference to
gender, her respect as a person with potential.

EMILIE BUCHWALD

I truly believe that if we put the strength
of our hearts and minds together that we can
change prejudice, and that my generation
of kids can grow up appreciating the
glorious rainbow of diversity.

SOL KELLEY-JONES

I look to a time when brotherhood needs no publicity;
to a time when a brotherhood award would be as
ridiculous as an award for getting up each morning.

DANIEL D. MICH

It is time for parents to teach young
people early on that in diversity there
is beauty and there is strength.

MAYA ANGELOU

As the sun illuminates the moon and stars,
so let us illuminate one another.

UNKNOWN

There is in each of us so much
goodness that if we could see its
glow, it would light the world.

SAM FRIEND

We're a great heart people.

PEARL BAILEY

Diversity in the world is a basic characteristic
of human society, and also the key condition
for a lively and dynamic world as we see today.

JINTAO HU

Just as we welcome a world of diversity,
so we glory in an America of diversity—
an America all the richer for the many different
and distinctive strands of which it is woven.

HUBERT HUMPHREY

We will create and sustain an inclusive environment
where all people regardless of race, gender, age,
ethnicity, religious beliefs, physical ability or sexual
orientation are challenged to achieve their full potential.

"DIVERSITY AND INCLUSION MISSION," SARALEE

I believe the greatest gift I can conceive of having from anyone is to be seen, heard, understood and touched by them. The greatest gift I can give is to see, hear, understand and touch another person.

VIRGINIA SATIR

When you begin to touch your heart or let your heart be touched, you begin to discover that it's bottomless, that it doesn't have any resolution, that this heart is huge, vast, and limitless. You begin to discover how much warmth and gentleness is there, as well as how much space.

PEMA CHODRON

If each person in this world will simply take a small piece of this huge thing, this amazing quilt, and work it regardless of the color of the yarn, we will have harmony on this planet.

CICELY TYSON

DIVERSITY

When we seek connection, we restore the world
to wholeness. Our seemingly separate lives become
meaningful as we discover how truly necessary
we are to each other.

MARGARET WHEATLEY

What I am is a humanist before anything—
before I'm a Jew, before I'm black, before I'm
a woman. And my beliefs are for the human
race—they don't exclude anyone.

WHOOPI GOLDBERG

What I'm calling humanism starts with the capacity
to *identify with*. It asks what we have in common
with others, while acknowledging the diversity among
ourselves. It is about the promise of shared humanity.

HENRY LOUIS GATES, JR.

We are not human beings on a spiritual journey.
We are spiritual beings on a human journey.

STEPHEN R. COVEY

Our creator rejoices in diversity and variety.
Any observation of our abundant earth and
its incredibly different life-forms proves this.

ROBYN KNIBBE

I think we're here for each other.

CAROL BURNETT

There is no feeling in a human heart which
exists in that heart alone—which is not,
in some form or degree, in every heart.

GEORGE MACDONALD

You are not only good to yourself,
but the cause of goodness in others.

SOCRATES

We are responsible for one another.

BETTY EADIE

What I do you cannot do; but what you do, I cannot do.
The needs are great, and none of us ever do great things.
But we can do small things, with great love, and together
we can do something wonderful.

MOTHER TERESA

I take as my guide the hope of a saint:
in crucial things, unity; in important things,
diversity; in all things, generosity.

GEORGE H. W. BUSH

One by one, we can be
the better world we wish for.

KOBI YAMADA

The common gift of humanity is that
we are all hard-wired to solve problems
by creating new solutions.

JOHN KOTEN

Each time we fit things together we are creating—
whether it is to make a loaf of bread, a child,
a day, a company, or a world.

CORITA KENT

The path to greatness is along with others.

BALTASAR GRACION

This could be such a beautiful world.

ROSALIND WELCHER

There is a destiny that makes us brothers,
no one goes his way alone; all that we send
into the lives of others, comes back into our own.

EDWIN MARKHAM

You have a unique message to deliver, a unique
song to sing, a unique act of love to bestow.
This message, this song, and this act of love
have been entrusted to the one and only you.

JOHN POWELL, S.J.

Embracing diversity is one adventure after another,
opening new paths of discovery that connect an
understanding to caring, listening, and sharing
with others who are different than ourselves.

APRIL HOLLAND

In our companies and communities we act—
together—as trustees for the future of our planet
and our children. We must act accordingly.

DOUGLAS K. SMITH

When building a great team, company or
community, four values are mentioned most
often: Honesty and openness in all dealings,
Respect for others, Service to others, and
Courage to act and live by convictions.

GEORGE MANNING

Great companies respect their customers and
employees—people at all levels and from all backgrounds.
By showing respect for others, an organization or team
itself becomes respected. It rises in stature, and makes
a positive impact on the world.

JAMES COLLINS

We don't have to wait for some grand utopian
future. The future is an infinite succession of presents,
and to live now as we think human beings should
live, in defiance of all that is bad around us,
is itself a marvelous victory.

HOWARD ZINN

We're all trying to make a big difference,
not realizing the small difference we make
for each other every day.

DAPHNE ROSE KINGMA

The key is to trust your own heart, as well as the hearts
of those around you, to move where your unique talents
can flourish. This old world will really spin when work
becomes a joyous expression of the soul.

AL SACHAROV

You are the people who are
shaping a better world.

THE DALAI LAMA

God has given each one of us approximately 26,000 days
on this earth. I truly believe He has something very specific
in mind: 8,300 days to sleep, 8,300 to work, and 8,300
to give, live, play, pray and love one another.

QUINCY JONES

Person to person, moment to moment,
as we love, we change the world.

SAMAHRIA LYTE KAUFMAN

We can make
a difference.
We can change
the world.
Because we are
the difference.
We are the world.

FREDERICO PEÑA

DIVERSITY

Other "Gift of Inspiration" books available:

Be Happy
**Remember to live, love,
laugh and learn**

Be the Difference

Because of You
Celebrating the Difference You Make

Brilliance
**Uncommon voices from
uncommon women**

Commitment to Excellence
Celebrating the Very Best

Everyone Leads
**It takes each of us to make
a difference for all of us**

Expect Success
Our Commitment to Our Customer

Forever Remembered
A Gift for the Grieving Heart

I Believe in You
**To your heart, your dream, and the
difference you make**

Little Miracles
**Cherished messages of hope, joy,
love, kindness and courage**

Reach for the Stars
**Give up the good to go
for the great**

Team Works
Working Together Works

Thank You
**In appreciation of you,
and all that you do**

To Your Success
**Thoughts to Give Wings to
Your Work and Your Dreams**

Together We Can
**Celebrating the power of
a team and a dream**

Welcome Home
**Celebrating the Best
Place on Earth**

What's Next
Creating the Future Now

Whatever It Takes
**A Journey into the Heart
of Human Achievement**

You've Got a Friend
**Thoughts to Celebrate
the Joy of Friendship**